The Strange & Beautiful Life of
DANIEL RASKOVICH

The Strange & Beautiful Life of
DANIEL RASKOVICH

Victor David Sandiego

MoonPath Press

Cover Photo & Interior Photos: Ethan Hahn
Author Photo: Mona Taleb

Design by Tonya Namura
using Fontin Sans and Optima

MoonPath Press is dedicated to
publishing the best poets of
the U.S. Pacific Northwest

MoonPath Press
PO Box 1808
Kingston, Washington 98346

MoonPathPress@yahoo.com

http://MoonPathPress.com

.

I dedicate this collection to the man with his fist turned up, his wrist bent back and his crooked eye sombrero in the too much sun. We passed on Calle Correo in early October as my head was occupied with morning coffee thoughts. In that brief encounter, I rediscovered a remarkable but often overlooked feature of creation.

Contents

The Strange & Beautiful Life of
DANIEL RASKOVICH

The birth of Daniel Raskovich

Just before midnight
Daniel put his hand out of the womb
like you do when you are not sure if it is raining.

Feeling his fingers go numb, he pulled them
back inside
and tucked himself into the fetal position.

When his mother kicked him in the rump
and told him to get out, headfirst
he screamed

(the few baby obscenities he knew)

but this did no good
since his mouth was filled with water.

Daniel Raskovich goes to school

Daniel was 7 years old
when his school in Cincinnati
burned down.

Luckily, all the teachers
were out with the flu, so only janitors
were in the building.

They escaped by dousing themselves
with mop water
and running through the flames.

Daniel was playing hooky, and saw
the whole thing from the bushes
through his new binoculars.

Daniel Raskovich and the assassination

Another time, all the kids at school started singing:

"President is dead, shot in the head!"

and Daniel ran home
as fast as he could to tell his mother.

At first, she scolded Daniel for playing tricks on her
but he hopped up and down and promised!
it was true.

When the television came on, the goldfish
that lived in a bowl on top of it kept swimming around
as usual…

but Daniel's mother got very still
and did not go back to washing her hair for a long time.

Random habits of Daniel Raskovich

Whenever there is a train wreck, Daniel looks
the other way.

He never goes to the bathroom on Wednesday.

He sets his clocks ahead one hour every night
and always brushes his teeth with two hands.

Anytime someone pops a balloon, he says:

"Bless you, my son!"

and even if he has only one more page to go
at bedtime
he turns off the light.

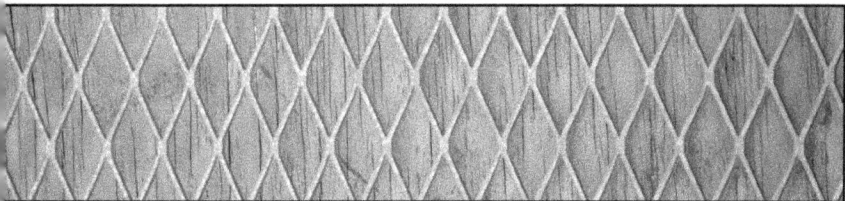

Daniel Raskovich finds a match

One late night, when Daniel was 9 years old
he was still thinking of the vampire movie
and went into his father's study
to look for a stake.

Under the divorce papers
he found his first wooden match
but it took three tries
before he could light it on the slick mahogany desk.

Later, when the firemen returned to the station
Daniel was reaching out the window
from the back seat of a gray sedan
to catch moths in his hands.

Daniel Raskovich gets dressed

In case anybody is watching
Daniel always puts his socks on from left to right.

This way too, if his house ever catches fire again
before he is finished
and there is snow on the ground
he can hop around on his good foot.

Daniel Raskovich goes shopping

When the stores open, Daniel pushes his cart
straight to the toothpaste aisle.

As a child, he was told
that only those with clean teeth
can go to heaven.

When he is done shopping
Daniel puts the receipt into his shirt pocket
close to his heart
takes the #21 back home
locks all the doors
and looks in the mirror.

Daniel Raskovich and the priest

One day in church, the priest
cornered Daniel in the restroom
and asked him about the missing collection plate.

Most mornings Daniel would have let the priest
have his way, but today
Daniel was feeling indestructible
on account of his big win at the dog races.

When the priest sniffed Daniel's left pants pocket
for the smell of silver, this upset Daniel;
he pulled the porcelain handle down
with a firm gesture, and walked back to his pew.

Daniel Raskovich and the president

When the president came to Cincinnati
to cut the ribbon for the new plastic bag factory
Daniel got up early to get in line
for an autograph.

As he was passing through the metal detector
it began to beep
because Daniel had a meat loaf sandwich
wrapped in foil in his pocket
as a gift.

At first, they thought Daniel was an assassin
but they let him through, after he took a bite
to prove the sandwich was harmless
and dribbled a little cranberry
on his shirt.

Jobs that didn't work out for Daniel Raskovich

Daniel always wanted to be a fireman
but he couldn't carry somebody
down six flights of stairs. He tried pushing
them out of the window instead, but they told him
that didn't count.

For a while, Daniel was a bookkeeper;
but the numbers had to be lined up neatly
and this reminded Daniel of toy soldiers.

When he was an ice cream vendor
Daniel gave cones
to kids with sad faces and no money.

This made the kids happy but his boss got mad
and fired him. The boss said:

"Kids are people, too."

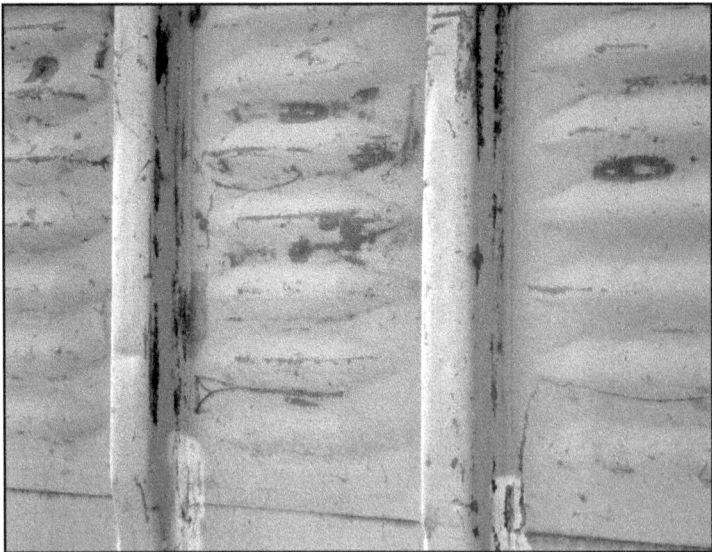

Daniel Raskovich learns a life lesson

One day, at the Greyhound station
Daniel saw a guy in a raincoat
with no underwear
screaming at the top of his voice about witches.

Daniel wasn't sure
if he should feel sad for this man
or pretend to read the schedule for Denver.

When an old lady backed out of the door
with her cheeks on fire
Daniel decided to compromise.

He got change for a ten, bought two candy bars
and a can of cola.

Daniel Raskovich in the news

Another day, Daniel tripped on an umbrella
some old guy had dropped on the sidewalk
during his heart attack.

Daniel tried to recover his balance
but he was halfway to the ground
before he remembered how.

Luckily, he landed on a skateboard
that had been missing for two days
and rolled under a waiting bus.

It was there he discovered the loose muffler
than could have killed everyone on board
with CO_2 poisoning.

Daniel Raskovich in love

When the girl approached him on W. Liberty St.
for spare change, Daniel thought
she was the most beautiful creature
he had ever seen.

Every day after that, for a week
he went to the bank to get a roll of quarters.

When his savings ran out
the girl took her carton of Camel Lights
and hitched a ride to Texas with a punk
rock drummer.

Daniel Raskovich gets a kiss

Nobody ever told Daniel that you were supposed
to wait for the drive-in movie to start.

He jumped right in with a joke his friends
said would impress her.

She didn't seem to get it, so he stretched out
his fingers
to let her know he was ready.

Pretty soon, she was licking the popcorn salt
from her lips, and giving Daniel sideways glances.

He was just about to take the plunge
when the speaker started crackling
and threw off his timing.

Daniel decided to wait until intermission
when he could look at the speaker
with a screwdriver.

But she said no, and turned the sound down
just as all the horses on the screen
began to buck their riders.

Daniel Raskovich has some spare time

In the summer
Daniel likes to walk around Cincinnati
with milk cartons, looking for kids.

Most of them just pretend he isn't there
but some of them call him names
and pull on his shoe laces.

Once, he thought for sure he spotted a familiar face!

Daniel ran to a streetlight to read the 800 number
but then he noticed the boy was too short
and his skin color was wrong.

Daniel Raskovich tries to join a club

One day a man downtown wearing a wool hat
asked Daniel if he wanted to join a club.

Daniel had never been in a club before
so he said yes.

When they got to the clubhouse, Daniel saw
that everyone was wearing red pants.

When he asked about that, they said
"Yes, it is something like a secret handshake
that only we can see."

All of Daniel's pants were green or blue
but he was embarrassed to admit that…
so he told them he couldn't afford the dues.

Daniel Raskovich saves the day

Daniel had a temp job walking the circus elephants
at the end of the day, because they get afraid
when the sun starts to get bigger
so far from home.

As they passed the liquor store
Daniel saw a man in an old Halloween mask
and the little immigrant man who owned the store
was bleeding! from a shoulder wound.

Daniel grabbed his bag and scoop
and rushed in.

The man in the mask tried to run away
but the stench overpowered him.

Daniel got a police citation and a coupon
for free ice cream.

Daniel Raskovich gets wet

On Tuesday nights, Daniel usually
walks down to the museum to count the cracks
in the vases.

This time, he forgot his umbrella and a taxi
splashed his shoes.

They don't let anyone into the museum
with wet feet

so Daniel had to wait by a heating grate
until he dried.

By then, the reception was over;
he went to the strip joint across the street
instead.

When the girls came on, Daniel took out a $5 bill
and licked it.

Daniel Raskovich and the gunman

One night, Daniel couldn't sleep;
he was so worried
that he might not win the sweepstakes drawing.

He took the #21 downtown
and started counting homeless people.

As he passed the parking lot of a bar
he heard loud voices and gunshots.

He rushed to the back of the lot
and threw himself on the gunman before he shot
any more beer bottles from the fence.

When the police came, they asked Daniel
why he did such a foolish thing.

"I was thirsty", Daniel said.

Daniel Raskovich goes fishing

When his freezer conked out, Daniel ran
out of chicken pot pies, and was forced
to fend for himself until the repairman came.

Fortunately, he had purchased a gold fish
during the last blackout that had now grown
to twice! its original size.

While the pan was heating, Daniel ran
down the street to the little Asian grocery store
and bought a bag of chips.

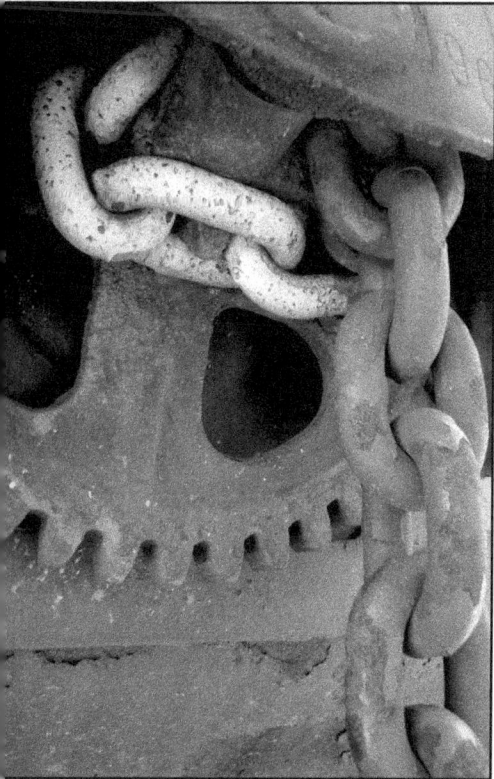

Daniel Raskovich on (prescription) drugs

Sometimes, Daniel calls the police on himself;
they arrive in a squad car with white wall tires
shoot chips in the brickwork façade of his house
to pass the time while they write him another ticket
for disturbing the peace. Then they shake their hats
back and forth, and grouse.

Daniel lost his position as restroom attendant
when a recession
hit the part of downtown Cincinnati
that specializes in medium priced hookers.

He told the review board, he was going to cause:
a legal ruckus!

but before he could proceed
his autistic mother moved in with him

(she brought three cats)

and after that: all he could think about
was the phone number of the precinct.

Daniel Raskovich goes to war

Daniel heard that if he didn't enlist at once
he'd have to learn a new language
that didn't have a word for cotton candy.

When the plane landed, it was hot
and everybody started to tell Daniel
the best way to polish bullets.

After he found his helmet, Daniel walked over
to the fence, and asked the squinty guy
on the other side
why they were fighting.

The squinty guy just pointed down
and Daniel couldn't figure out what he meant.

The next time Daniel woke up, he wrapped
his rifle in a blanket. Then he ate breakfast
while reading the artillery map.

Sometimes, the flares hurt his eyes
but Daniel was afraid to admit this
so he just pretended they were church candles.

If a crater was full, Daniel waited his turn.
He always combed his hair before he ran downhill.

When the bodies ran out, they told Daniel
to pick up his rations, and go home.

On the way out, he stopped for a new grenade pin
to replace the one he had lost.

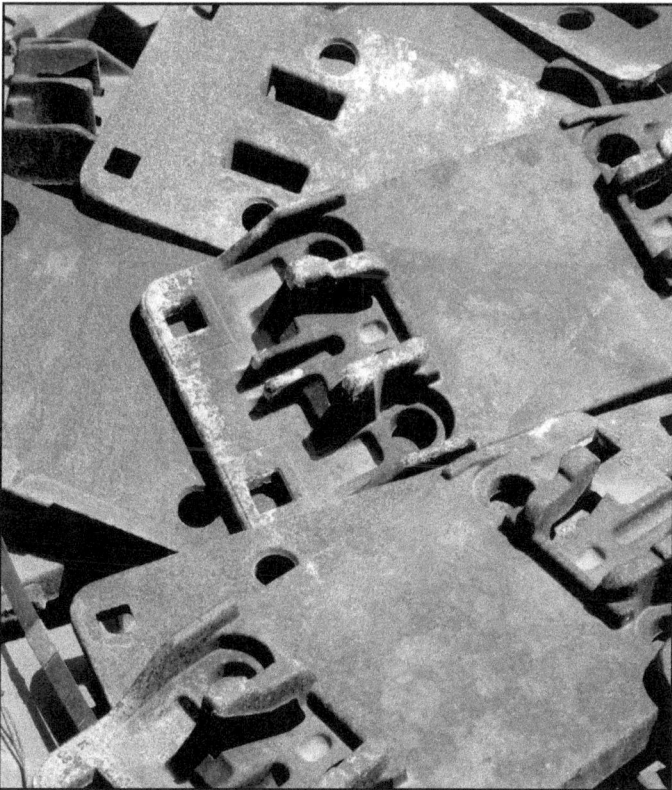

Daniel Raskovich in mourning

This time, Daniel remembered to bring a hammer
and a box of nails to the funeral.

While everyone was eating cupcakes
he pried open the coffin to make sure his father
was dead.

His father had two glass eyes
and used to let Daniel
tap on them with a ballpoint pen.

When Daniel was small, his father
always gave him a bath in the washing machine.
They didn't have a dryer.

As he lowered the lid, Daniel remembered
just the day before
he had mailed his father a birthday card.

Eulogy for Daniel Raskovich

The only time
that Daniel got to ride in the back of an ambulance
screeching through the streets of Cincinnati
he was almost dead.

He tried to speak
but his tongue kept bouncing into his teeth.

It wasn't until all the candles were lit
that his wound became apparent.

"A blunt blow, to the head, with a limb of oak."
said the priest.

Daniel always loved to climb a tree.

41

Victor David Sandiego is a poet/drummer/composer who divides his time between México, Central America, and the Pacific Northwest. He was the winner of the 1st WordStorm Poetry Competition held on Vancouver Island in British Columbia, a winner of the 2008 Jeanne Lohmann Poetry Prize, and the winner of the 2009 *Crab Creek Review* poetry contest. He is the author of several poetry books and his work has appeared (or is upcoming) in *Floating Bridge Review, Crab Creek Review, Cascade, Grasslimb, Cerise Press, Prime Number* and on public radio. More at: www.VictorDavid.com.

Ethan Hahn is a musician, artist, and occasional photographer. After spending a few years in Denton, Texas, as a part-time musician and obtaining his B.S., he's back in his hometown Denver, Colorado. When Ethan is not creating art from recycled materials, he enjoys researching live music and obscure bands. He runs a local music resource website at www.soundplot.net.

www.ingramcontent.com/pod-product-compliance
Lightning Source LLC
Chambersburg PA
CBHW072038060426
42449CB00010BA/2331